Calm as Ever

Black Women Self Care Journal

CALM AS EVER: BLACK WOMEN SELF CARE JOURNAL

ISBN: 978-1-7348797-5-9

For more information, visit us online at www.entrepreneurscolortoo.com

What's Included In this Journal

Section 1 - Weekly Tracker with 90 Days to plan your Self Care Routine and brainstorm ideas that you would like to focus on. This allows you to ask yourself questions about your week and then implement a Self Care Strategy into your day.

Section 2- Creative Activities and Guided Prompts to help you discover more about yourself in a deeper way.

Section 3- Free space for Personal Reflections to continue focusing on making yourself a priority. Each page also includes inspirational quotes and affirmations.

What is Self Care?

Self Care means you are recognizing the relationship you have with yourself and prioritizing it – this means you have to put in intentional effort and keep it going. Sometimes it also means calling ourselves out on the things we are doing that aren't healthy for us.

What is a Self Care Plan?

A Self Care Plan helps you establish a routine and have a roadmap in place that encourages you to take a step back to breathe, refocus and make yourself a priority. Effective self care is holistic and helps you mentally, physically, emotionally and socially in order to focus on your whole self.

Everyone's self care needs are different but let's begin the journal by taking time out to write a letter to yourself. Write down some positive things you want to say to yourself, just like how you would to your best friend or a family member. Read the letter anytime you need a little pick me up.

Sometimes you have to encourage yourself sis!

Begin your letter on the next page...

NOTE TO SELF

_____

Dear _____,

_____

_____

_____

_____

_____

_____

xo, _____

If I am not good to myself, how can I expect anyone else to be good to me?

- Maya Angelou

Weekly Self Care Tracker

Week of: 1/10/21

Self Care Goals:

-DEVELOP A REGULAR SLEEP ROUTINE

-AIM FOR A HEALTHY DIET

-TAKE MY FULL LUNCH BREAK

-GO FOR A WALK DURING LUNCH

Steps I'll take:

-SET A BEDTIME THAT'S EARLY ENOUGH TO GET AT LEAST 7 HOURS OF SLEEP

-RESEARCH SOME HEALTHY MEALS THAT I MAY LIKE

-SET MY ALARM AS A TIMER

-FIND A ROUTE AND BRING SNEAKERS

What didn't work well last week:

WAS WAY TOO OVERWHELMED SO ENDED UP SHUTTING DOWN AND NOT GETTING ANYTHING DONE.

Best part of last week:

MY DOGS SURGERY WENT WELL.

What I'm looking forward to this week:

GETTING SOME TIME TO RELAX AND WATCH A NEW MOVIE COMING OUT ON NETFLIX.

Sample Page

MONDAY
- LAST DAY OF TRAINING ✓
- PACK ORDERS ✓ ✓
- CALL GRANDMA ✓

TUESDAY
- DR'S APPT AT 1PM ✓
- VIDEO CHAT
- READING

WEDNESDAY
- CLEAN UP ✓
- HOMEWORK
- GROCERY SHOPPING

THURSDAY
- WASH DISHES ✓
- DRAW
- CHAT W/MOM ✓

FRIDAY
- TAKE OFF WORK ✓
- CAR TO THE SHOP
- COOK SPAGHETTI

SATURDAY
- LOOK FOR NEW CAR
- MEDITATE
- EXERCISE

SUNDAY
- PRAY ✓
- WASH CLOTHES
- VIRTUAL CHURCH

Choose a habit that you would like to keep track of this week

HABIT TRACKER

TOOK MEDS

M ✓   T   W ✓   T ✓   F ✓   S ✓   S

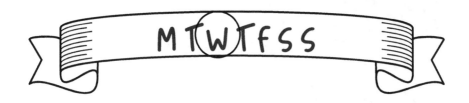

MTWTFSS

How do you feel right now?

FEELING REALLY ACCOMPLISHED!

What are you grateful for today?

HAVING A JOB AND INCOME TO PAY BILLS.

Reflection of the day:

TODAY I WAS ABLE TO REALLY FOCUS ON ME AND MY PRIORITIES.

Today's Encouraging Scripture or Quote:

I CAN DO ALL THINGS THROUGH CHRIST WHO STRENGTHENS ME. - PHIL 4:13

 Water:

Weekly
Self Care
Tracker

Week of:

Self Care Goals:

Steps I'll take:

What didn't work well last week:

Best part of last week:

What I'm looking forward to this week:

Choose a habit that you would like to keep track of this week

HABIT TRACKER

M   T   W   T   F   S   S

MTWTFSS

How do you feel right now?

What are you grateful for today?

Reflection of the day:

Today's Encouraging Scripture or Quote:

Water:

MTWTFSS

How do you feel right now?

What are you grateful for today?

Reflection of the day:

Today's Encouraging Scripture or Quote:

 Water:

MTWTFSS

How do you feel right now?

What are you grateful for today?

Reflection of the day:

Today's Encouraging Scripture or Quote:

Water:

MTWTFSS

How do you feel right now?

What are you grateful for today?

Reflection of the day:

Today's Encouraging Scripture or Quote:

 Water:

MTWTFSS

How do you feel right now?

What are you grateful for today?

Reflection of the day:

Today's Encouraging Scripture or Quote:

Water:

MTWTFSS

How do you feel right now?

What are you grateful for today?

Reflection of the day:

Today's Encouraging Scripture or Quote:

 Water:

MTWTFSS

How do you feel right now?

What are you grateful for today?

Reflection of the day:

Today's Encouraging Scripture or Quote:

Water:

Weekly Self Care Tracker

Week of:

Self Care Goals:

Steps I'll take:

What didn't work well last week:

Best part of last week:

What I'm looking forward to this week:

Choose a habit that you would like to keep track of this week

HABIT TRACKER

M T W T F S S

MTWTFSS

How do you feel right now?

What are you grateful for today?

Reflection of the day:

Today's Encouraging Scripture or Quote:

Water:

MTWTFSS

How do you feel right now?

What are you grateful for today?

Reflection of the day:

Today's Encouraging Scripture or Quote:

Water:

MTWTFSS

How do you feel right now?

What are you grateful for today?

Reflection of the day:

Today's Encouraging Scripture or Quote:

Water:

MTWTFSS

How do you feel right now?

What are you grateful for today?

Reflection of the day:

Today's Encouraging Scripture or Quote:

Water:

Weekly Self Care Tracker

Week of:

Self Care Goals:

Steps I'll take:

What didn't work well last week:

Best part of last week:

What I'm looking forward to this week:

Choose a habit that you would like to keep track of this week

HABIT TRACKER

M   T   W   T   F   S   S

MTWTFSS

How do you feel right now?

What are you grateful for today?

Reflection of the day:

Today's Encouraging Scripture or Quote:

Water:

MTWTFSS

How do you feel right now?

What are you grateful for today?

Reflection of the day:

Today's Encouraging Scripture or Quote:

Water:

MTWTFSS

How do you feel right now?

What are you grateful for today?

Reflection of the day:

Today's Encouraging Scripture or Quote:

Water:

MTWTFSS

How do you feel right now?

What are you grateful for today?

Reflection of the day:

Today's Encouraging Scripture or Quote:

Water:

MTWTFSS

How do you feel right now?

What are you grateful for today?

Reflection of the day:

Today's Encouraging Scripture or Quote:

Water:

MTWTFSS

How do you feel right now?

What are you grateful for today?

Reflection of the day:

Today's Encouraging Scripture or Quote:

Water:

MTWTFSS

How do you feel right now?

What are you grateful for today?

Reflection of the day:

Today's Encouraging Scripture or Quote:

Water:

Weekly Self Care Tracker

Week of:

Self Care Goals:

Steps I'll take:

What didn't work well last week:

Best part of last week:

What I'm looking forward to this week:

Date   /   /

Choose a habit that you would like to keep track of this week

HABIT TRACKER

M   T   W   T   F   S   S

MTWTFSS

How do you feel right now?

What are you grateful for today?

Reflection of the day:

Today's Encouraging Scripture or Quote:

Water:

MTWTFSS

How do you feel right now?

What are you grateful for today?

Reflection of the day:

Today's Encouraging Scripture or Quote:

 Water:

MTWTFSS

How do you feel right now?

What are you grateful for today?

Reflection of the day:

Today's Encouraging Scripture or Quote:

Water:

MTWTFSS

How do you feel right now?

What are you grateful for today?

Reflection of the day:

Today's Encouraging Scripture or Quote:

Water:

MTWTFSS

How do you feel right now?

What are you grateful for today?

Reflection of the day:

Today's Encouraging Scripture or Quote:

Water:

MTWTFSS

How do you feel right now?

What are you grateful for today?

Reflection of the day:

Today's Encouraging Scripture or Quote:

Water:

MTWTFSS

How do you feel right now?

What are you grateful for today?

Reflection of the day:

Today's Encouraging Scripture or Quote:

Water:

Weekly Self Care Tracker

Week of:

Self Care Goals:

Steps I'll take:

What didn't work well last week:

Best part of last week:

What I'm looking forward to this week:

Choose a habit that you would like to keep track of this week

HABIT TRACKER

M   T   W   T   F   S   S

MTWTFSS

How do you feel right now?

What are you grateful for today?

Reflection of the day:

Today's Encouraging Scripture or Quote:

 Water:

MTWTFSS

How do you feel right now?

What are you grateful for today?

Reflection of the day:

Today's Encouraging Scripture or Quote:

Water:

MTWTFSS

How do you feel right now?

What are you grateful for today?

Reflection of the day:

Today's Encouraging Scripture or Quote:

Water:

MTWTFSS

How do you feel right now?

What are you grateful for today?

Reflection of the day:

Today's Encouraging Scripture or Quote:

Water:

MTWTFSS

How do you feel right now?

What are you grateful for today?

Reflection of the day:

Today's Encouraging Scripture or Quote:

 Water:

MTWTFSS

How do you feel right now?

What are you grateful for today?

Reflection of the day:

Today's Encouraging Scripture or Quote:

Water:

MTWTFSS

How do you feel right now?

What are you grateful for today?

Reflection of the day:

Today's Encouraging Scripture or Quote:

Water:

Weekly Self Care Tracker

Week of:

Self Care Goals:

Steps I'll take:

What didn't work well last week:

Best part of last week:

What I'm looking forward to this week:

Choose a habit that you would like to keep track of this week

HABIT TRACKER

M   T   W   T   F   S   S

MTWTFSS

How do you feel right now?

What are you grateful for today?

Reflection of the day:

Today's Encouraging Scripture or Quote:

Water:

MTWTFSS

How do you feel right now?

What are you grateful for today?

Reflection of the day:

Today's Encouraging Scripture or Quote:

 Water:

MTWTFSS

How do you feel right now?

What are you grateful for today?

Reflection of the day:

Today's Encouraging Scripture or Quote:

Water:

MTWTFSS

How do you feel right now?

What are you grateful for today?

Reflection of the day:

Today's Encouraging Scripture or Quote:

Water:

MTWTFSS

How do you feel right now?

What are you grateful for today?

Reflection of the day:

Today's Encouraging Scripture or Quote:

Water:

MTWTFSS

How do you feel right now?

What are you grateful for today?

Reflection of the day:

Today's Encouraging Scripture or Quote:

 Water:

MTWTFSS

How do you feel right now?

What are you grateful for today?

Reflection of the day:

Today's Encouraging Scripture or Quote:

Water:

Weekly
Self Care
Tracker

Week of:

Self Care Goals: Steps I'll take:

What didn't work well last week:

Best part of last week:

What I'm looking forward to this week:

Choose a habit that you would like to keep track of this week

HABIT TRACKER

M T W T F S S

MTWTFSS

How do you feel right now?

What are you grateful for today?

Reflection of the day:

Today's Encouraging Scripture or Quote:

Water:

MTWTFSS

How do you feel right now?

What are you grateful for today?

Reflection of the day:

Today's Encouraging Scripture or Quote:

Water:

MTWTFSS

How do you feel right now?

What are you grateful for today?

Reflection of the day:

Today's Encouraging Scripture or Quote:

Water:

MTWTFSS

How do you feel right now?

What are you grateful for today?

Reflection of the day:

Today's Encouraging Scripture or Quote:

Water:

MTWTFSS

How do you feel right now?

What are you grateful for today?

Reflection of the day:

Today's Encouraging Scripture or Quote:

Water:

MTWTFSS

How do you feel right now?

What are you grateful for today?

Reflection of the day:

Today's Encouraging Scripture or Quote:

Water:

MTWTFSS

How do you feel right now?

What are you grateful for today?

Reflection of the day:

Today's Encouraging Scripture or Quote:

Water:

Weekly Self Care Tracker

Week of:

Self Care Goals:

Steps I'll take:

What didn't work well last week:

Best part of last week:

What I'm looking forward to this week:

Date   /   /

Choose a habit that you would like to keep track of this week

HABIT TRACKER

M   T   W   T   F   S   S

MTWTFSS

How do you feel right now?

What are you grateful for today?

Reflection of the day:

Today's Encouraging Scripture or Quote:

Water:

MTWTFSS

How do you feel right now?

What are you grateful for today?

Reflection of the day:

Today's Encouraging Scripture or Quote:

 Water:

MTWTFSS

How do you feel right now?

What are you grateful for today?

Reflection of the day:

Today's Encouraging Scripture or Quote:

Water:

MTWTFSS

How do you feel right now?

What are you grateful for today?

Reflection of the day:

Today's Encouraging Scripture or Quote:

Water:

MTWTFSS

How do you feel right now?

What are you grateful for today?

Reflection of the day:

Today's Encouraging Scripture or Quote:

Water:

MTWTFSS

How do you feel right now?

What are you grateful for today?

Reflection of the day:

Today's Encouraging Scripture or Quote:

Water:

MTWTFSS

How do you feel right now?

What are you grateful for today?

Reflection of the day:

Today's Encouraging Scripture or Quote:

Water:

Weekly Self Care Tracker

Week of:

Self Care Goals:

Steps I'll take:

What didn't work well last week:

Best part of last week:

What I'm looking forward to this week:

Date   /   /

Choose a habit that you would like to keep track of this week

HABIT TRACKER

M   T   W   T   F   S   S

MTWTFSS

How do you feel right now?

What are you grateful for today?

Reflection of the day:

Today's Encouraging Scripture or Quote:

Water:

MTWTFSS

How do you feel right now?

What are you grateful for today?

Reflection of the day:

Today's Encouraging Scripture or Quote:

Water:

MTWTFSS

How do you feel right now?

What are you grateful for today?

Reflection of the day:

Today's Encouraging Scripture or Quote:

Water:

MTWTFSS

How do you feel right now?

What are you grateful for today?

Reflection of the day:

Today's Encouraging Scripture or Quote:

Water:

MTWTFSS

How do you feel right now?

What are you grateful for today?

Reflection of the day:

Today's Encouraging Scripture or Quote:

 Water:

MTWTFSS

How do you feel right now?

What are you grateful for today?

Reflection of the day:

Today's Encouraging Scripture or Quote:

Water:

MTWTFSS

How do you feel right now?

What are you grateful for today?

Reflection of the day:

Today's Encouraging Scripture or Quote:

Water:

Weekly Self Care Tracker

Week of:

Self Care Goals:

Steps I'll take:

What didn't work well last week:

Best part of last week:

What I'm looking forward to this week:

Choose a habit that you would like to keep track of this week

MTWTFSS

How do you feel right now?

What are you grateful for today?

Reflection of the day:

Today's Encouraging Scripture or Quote:

Water:

MTWTFSS

How do you feel right now?

What are you grateful for today?

Reflection of the day:

Today's Encouraging Scripture or Quote:

Water:

MTWTFSS

How do you feel right now?

What are you grateful for today?

Reflection of the day:

Today's Encouraging Scripture or Quote:

Water:

MTWTFSS

How do you feel right now?

What are you grateful for today?

Reflection of the day:

Today's Encouraging Scripture or Quote:

Water:

MTWTFSS

How do you feel right now?

What are you grateful for today?

Reflection of the day:

Today's Encouraging Scripture or Quote:

Water:

MTWTFSS

How do you feel right now?

What are you grateful for today?

Reflection of the day:

Today's Encouraging Scripture or Quote:

Water:

MTWTFSS

How do you feel right now?

What are you grateful for today?

Reflection of the day:

Today's Encouraging Scripture or Quote:

Water:

Weekly Self Care Tracker

Week of:

Self Care Goals:

Steps I'll take:

What didn't work well last week:

Best part of last week:

What I'm looking forward to this week:

Choose a habit that you would like to keep track of this week

HABIT TRACKER

M   T   W   T   F   S   S

MTWTFSS

How do you feel right now?

What are you grateful for today?

Reflection of the day:

Today's Encouraging Scripture or Quote:

Water:

MTWTFSS

How do you feel right now?

What are you grateful for today?

Reflection of the day:

Today's Encouraging Scripture or Quote:

Water:

MTWTFSS

How do you feel right now?

What are you grateful for today?

Reflection of the day:

Today's Encouraging Scripture or Quote:

Water:

MTWTFSS

How do you feel right now?

What are you grateful for today?

Reflection of the day:

Today's Encouraging Scripture or Quote:

Water:

MTWTFSS

How do you feel right now?

What are you grateful for today?

Reflection of the day:

Today's Encouraging Scripture or Quote:

Water:

MTWTFSS

How do you feel right now?

What are you grateful for today?

Reflection of the day:

Today's Encouraging Scripture or Quote:

Water:

MTWTFSS

How do you feel right now?

What are you grateful for today?

Reflection of the day:

Today's Encouraging Scripture or Quote:

Water:

Weekly Self Care Tracker

Week of:

Self Care Goals:

Steps I'll take:

What didn't work well last week:

Best part of last week:

What I'm looking forward to this week:

Choose a habit that you would like to keep track of this week

HABIT TRACKER

M   T   W   T   F   S   S

MTWTFSS

How do you feel right now?

What are you grateful for today?

Reflection of the day:

Today's Encouraging Scripture or Quote:

Water:

MTWTFSS

How do you feel right now?

What are you grateful for today?

Reflection of the day:

Today's Encouraging Scripture or Quote:

Water:

MTWTFSS

How do you feel right now?

What are you grateful for today?

Reflection of the day:

Today's Encouraging Scripture or Quote:

Water:

MTWTFSS

How do you feel right now?

What are you grateful for today?

Reflection of the day:

Today's Encouraging Scripture or Quote:

Water:

MTWTFSS

How do you feel right now?

What are you grateful for today?

Reflection of the day:

Today's Encouraging Scripture or Quote:

Water:

MTWTFSS

How do you feel right now?

What are you grateful for today?

Reflection of the day:

Today's Encouraging Scripture or Quote:

Water:

MTWTFSS

How do you feel right now?

What are you grateful for today?

Reflection of the day:

Today's Encouraging Scripture or Quote:

Water:

Weekly Self Care Tracker

Week of:

Self Care Goals:

Steps I'll take:

What didn't work well last week:

Best part of last week:

What I'm looking forward to this week:

Choose a habit that you would like to keep track of this week

HABIT TRACKER

M   T   W   T   F   S   S

MTWTFSS

How do you feel right now?

What are you grateful for today?

Reflection of the day:

Today's Encouraging Scripture or Quote:

 Water:

MTWTFSS

How do you feel right now?

What are you grateful for today?

Reflection of the day:

Today's Encouraging Scripture or Quote:

Water:

MTWTFSS

How do you feel right now?

What are you grateful for today?

Reflection of the day:

Today's Encouraging Scripture or Quote:

Water:

MTWTFSS

How do you feel right now?

What are you grateful for today?

Reflection of the day:

Today's Encouraging Scripture or Quote:

Water:

MTWTFSS

How do you feel right now?

What are you grateful for today?

Reflection of the day:

Today's Encouraging Scripture or Quote:

Water:

MTWTFSS

How do you feel right now?

What are you grateful for today?

Reflection of the day:

Today's Encouraging Scripture or Quote:

Water:

MTWTFSS

How do you feel right now?

What are you grateful for today?

Reflection of the day:

Today's Encouraging Scripture or Quote:

Water:

SELF CARE
IS NOT
SELFISH

ALL ABOUT ME

I AM

YEARS OLD

I WEIGH

POUNDS

I STAND

INCHES TALL

MY FAV'S

COLOR:

ANIMAL:

FOOD:

MOVIE:

BOOK:

ACTIVITY:

SONG:

PLACE:

WHAT THINGS
MAKE YOU HAPPY?

1.

2.

3.

4.

5.

6.

What do you love about yourself?

What is something you always love doing, even when you are tired or rushed? Why?

If a relationship or job makes you unhappy, do you choose to stay or leave?

What have you done in your life that you are most proud of?

How is your relationship with money?

WHAT WOULD MAKE TODAY GREAT?

WHAT ARE SOME THINGS THAT INSPIRE YOU?

WHAT'S A FUNNY STORY THAT MAKES YOU LAUGH EVERYTIME?

WHAT ARE SOME HOBBIES YOU WANT TO TRY?

CREATIVE
WAYS TO TAKE A BREAK

COLOR ME

WHAT IS NO LONGER SERVING ME?

WHAT AM I TRULY NEEDING IN THIS PRESENT MOMENT?

WHAT IS STOPPING ME FROM GETTING WHAT I NEED?

TAPE SOME SPECIAL MEMORIES TO THIS PAGE

Do a worry purge on this page. Without stopping, write down everything that is going on in your mind at this moment.

Once you get it out on paper, give yourself permission to leave it in your journal and come back to it later with a clearer head.

WHAT MAKES
YOU FEEL LOVED?

HOW DO YOU
SHOW PEOPLE
YOU CARE?

WHAT MAKES
YOU CRY?

WHAT BUGS
YOU?

WRITE YOUR FAVORITE RECIPE

WHEN WAS THE LAST TIME YOU MADE THIS?

IF IT HAS BEEN A WHILE CAN YOU SET A DATE TO MAKE
IT SOON?

. . . .

WHAT IS SOMETHING YOU HAVE DONE THAT YOU'RE NOT PROUD OF? IF IT INVOLVED ANOTHER PERSON HAVE YOU FORGIVEN THEM? HAVE YOU FORGIVEN YOURSELF?

ONCE YOU WRITE IT SAY "I FORGIVE YOU FOR..."

NOW, RIP THIS PAGE OUT, BURN IT AND LET IT GO.

WHAT COLOR DOES STRESS FEEL LIKE TO ME?

NOW, WITH YOUR FAVORITE COLOR DRAW SOMETHING THAT HELPS YOU RELIEVE STRESS...

FINISH THE SENTENCE, "RIGHT NOW I AM..."

FINISH THE SENTENCE, "I WANT TO BE..."

DOODLE ON THIS PAGE

SIT QUIETLY FOR A MINUTE, JUST BREATHING AND LISTENING TO YOUR BODY. WHERE DO YOU FEEL STRONG, HEALTHY, RELAXED?

WHERE DO YOU FEEL TENSE, WORRIED, TIRED?

WHAT PART OF YOU IS ASKING FOR MORE ATTENTION?

WHAT IS ONE OF THE NICEST THINGS SOMEONE HAS DONE FOR YOU?

WHAT IS SOMETHING YOU WOULD LIKE TO LEARN HOW TO DO?

WHAT DO YOU NEED TO DO IN ORDER TO ACCOMPLISH IT?

CAN YOU TAKE THE FIRST STEP OF GETTING IT DONE TODAY?

YES   NO

BRAIN DUMP HERE.

SPRAY YOUR FAVORITE SMELL HERE

HAVE A HEART TO HEART WITH THE THOUGHTS YOU ARE HEARING. IF THEY HAVE BEEN EXTRA LOUD AND VOCAL TODAY TELLING YOU ALL THE THINGS YOU ARE DOING WRONG, TAKE A MOMENT TO REPLY BACK WITH ALL THE THINGS YOU ARE DOING RIGHT.

THINK OF ONE PERSON WHO HAS MADE YOUR WORLD A LITTLE BIT BETTER RECENTLY. WRITE DOWN THE FEELING THEY GIVE YOU IN ONE WORD OR TWO.

GET OUT YOUR COLORED PENCILS AND DECORATE THE REST OF THIS PAGE WITH FLOWERS.

IF YOU HAVE BEEN ESPECIALLY HARD ON YOURSELF, WRITE YOURSELF AN APOLOGY NOTE...

IF YOU HAVEN'T THEN SKIP THIS PAGE

PICK A POSITIVE WORD THAT YOU WANT TO FOCUS ON TODAY - SUCH AS LOVE, PEACE OR FORGIVENESS. JOURNAL ABOUT ALL THE WAYS YOU HAVE EXPERIENCED THIS WORD LATELY AND ALL THE WAYS YOU WANT TO.

CHOOSE ONE PROBLEM THAT HAS BEEN CAUSING YOU ANXIETY LATELY, AND ASK YOURSELF QUESTIONS ABOUT IT, THE WAY A CLOSE FRIEND WOULD. TRY LOOKING AT THE SITUATION FROM NEW ANGLES, AND BE OPEN TO POSSIBLE SOLUTIONS THAT COME UP.

Self-Care Check-List

CHECK THE BOXES OF THE ACTIVITIES YOU HAVE DONE WITHIN THE PAST 7 DAYS TO TAKE CARE OF YOURSELF.

- [ ] Color
- [ ] Take a break from everything
- [ ] Find a quiet spot to meditate
- [ ] Light a good smelling candle
- [ ] Do a gratitude list
- [ ] Practice deep breathing
- [ ] Listen to good music
- [ ] Exercise
- [ ] Draw
- [ ] Visit a family member
- [ ] Spend time outdoors
- [ ] Have a mini pamper session
- [ ] Cuddle a pet
- [ ] Try something new

MY SIGNS OF BURNOUT

THINGS THAT CALM ME DOWN

PEOPLE I CAN REACH OUT TO FOR SUPPORT

30 DAY
SELF CARE
CHALLENGE

Day 1- Go for a 15 min walk	Day 2- Stay off social media for 1 hour	Day 3- Take a bubble bath	Day 4- Book your yearly physical	Day 5- Watch a movie alone
Day 6- Do something you love	Day 7- Unfollow negative people	Day 8- Frame a photo from your phone	Day 9- Listen to a soothing podcast	Day 10- Meditate 10 minutes before bed
Day 11- Figure out something yourself	Day 12- Take a Mental Health Day	Day 13- Eat lunch anywhere but your desk	Day 14- Listen to your fav childhood album	Day 15- Spend 30 mins doing something creative
Day 16- Catch up with an old friend or relative	Day 17- Get a massage	Day 18- Forgive Someone	Day 19- Try Something New w/ your hair	Day 20- Random Act of Kindness
Day 21- Stretch your entire body	Day 22- Watch a Documentary	Day 23- Eat a Healthy Lunch	Day 24- Do something you've been putting off	Day 25- Create a list of long term goals
Day 26- Define what gives you stress	Day 27- Organize your desk	Day 28- Start a new book	Day 29- Write in your journal	Day 30- Try a New Recipe

ASK FOR WHAT YOU NEED EVEN IF IT SCARES YOU TO VOICE IT

PERSONAL REFLECTIONS

I AM BEAUIFUL

PERSONAL REFLECTIONS

GIVE YOUR MIND TIME TO UNWIND

PERSONAL REFLECTIONS

IT'S OK TO HAVE BAD DAYS

PERSONAL REFLECTIONS

YOU MATTER

PERSONAL REFLECTIONS

BE KIND TO YOU

PERSONAL REFLECTIONS

SELF CARE IS SELF LOVE

PERSONAL REFLECTIONS

I AM ALLOWED TO SAY NO

PERSONAL REFLECTIONS

SELF CARE IS NOT SELFISH

PERSONAL REFLECTIONS

DON'T BE AFRAID TO SAY YES

PERSONAL REFLECTIONS

LET GO OF WHAT YOU CAN'T CONTROL

PERSONAL REFLECTIONS

_____

_____

_____

_____

_____

_____

_____

_____

_____

_____

_____

_____

_____

_____

STAY AWAY FROM NEGATIVITY

PERSONAL REFLECTIONS

LOVE

PERSONAL REFLECTIONS

YOU ARE HERE FOR A REASON

PERSONAL REFLECTIONS

CELEBRATE YOURSELF

PERSONAL REFLECTIONS

DON'T COMPARE YOURSELF TO OTHERS

PERSONAL REFLECTIONS

LET GO OF PAST MISTAKES

PERSONAL REFLECTIONS

SLOW DOWN AND BE PRESENT

PERSONAL REFLECTIONS

BREATHE SIS

PERSONAL REFLECTIONS

NEVER GIVE UP

PERSONAL REFLECTIONS

DON'T BE A PEOPLE PLEASURE

PERSONAL REFLECTIONS

SAY EXACTLY WHAT YOU MEAN

PERSONAL REFLECTIONS

HEAVY ON THE SELF LOVE

PERSONAL REFLECTIONS

YOU DESERVE GOOD THINGS

PERSONAL REFLECTIONS

MENTAL HEALTH IS JUST AS IMPORTANT AS PHYSICAL HEALTH

PERSONAL REFLECTIONS

YOUR STORY MATTERS

PERSONAL REFLECTIONS

IT RAN IN MY FAMILY UNTIL IT RAN INTO ME

PERSONAL REFLECTIONS

MY ALONE TIME IS FOR EVERYONE'S BENEFIT

PERSONAL REFLECTIONS

THE BEST DAYS OF MY LIFE ARE AHEAD OF ME

PERSONAL REFLECTIONS

RELAX SIS, YOU'RE GOING TO MAKE IT

PERSONAL REFLECTIONS

I AM CALM AND AT PEACE

THIS IS
JUST THE
BEGINNING!

KEEP MAKING
YOURSELF A
PRIORITY!

CPSIA information can be obtained
at www.ICGtesting.com
Printed in the USA
LVHW080530051122
732363LV00008B/252

9 781734 879759